Making Conscious Decisions to Land on Your Feet

Choose yourself every day. You deserve it.

Dr. Aldith D. Campbell,Ed.D

ISBN 978-93-5610-888-2
© Dr. Aldith D. Campbell,Ed.D 2022
Published in India 2022 by Pencil

A brand of

One Point Six Technologies Pvt. Ltd.
123, Building J2, Shram Seva Premises,
Wadala Truck Terminal, Wadala (E)
Mumbai 400037, Maharashtra, INDIA
E connect@thepencilapp.com
W www.thepencilapp.com

DISCLAIMER: *The opinions expressed in this book are those of the authors and do not purport to reflect the views of the Publisher.*

Author biography

I earned my BA at Wilkes University in Communications, MBA from the University of Phoenix in Health Care Management, and my Doctorate from Argosy University in Counseling Psychology. I am a Leader, Mentor, and Business Owner, who has dedicated my career to helping others in higher education, mental health as well as workforce development.

CONTENTS

Preface

DR CAMPBELL seeks to inspire, motivate, and empower her readers to find their inner greatness.
NEVER GIVE UP ON YOURSELF

Introduction

Sometimes life takes you through hills and valleys before you reach your true destiny. It is never a time to give up but a time to fight. No race is the same, therefore each runner will take a different course. Choose your path and walk it your way. The formula for success does not come in one bottle because it is designed with more than one hand. Find the hand that fits you and hold on to it. Then make it unique to you.

Remain Humble

Remain humble throughout your trials and tribulations. Take notice of the things that kept you from moving forward and learn from them. Be mindful of the choices you make while working through your already made mistakes. While you are going through the transition and trying to move forward, do not focus on the loss that you suffered too much because it will hinder you from moving forward all over again. Know that you are a gem. You were born for a purpose. Know that your purpose is still being fulfilled and that you belong to yourself and no one else.

The world is full of opinions and people are always going to judge you, but that does not signify that what they are saying is true. Opinions will come and go because if you are breathing and trying to make something of yourself, there will be someone who finds it ok to disrespect you or try to destroy what you are trying to build.

So now that you have accepted the fact that you will always be talked about, go out and make a life for yourself. Aspire to be even greater than your haters thought you would be. Take that chance that you have always been afraid of because you are afraid of that word, we call failure. Do not be afraid to fail. Some of your biggest failures will become your greatest asset.

Trusting Yourself Even When Life Looks Bad

When you trust yourself even in your darkest hour, you begin to find out all the things that you like about yourself and the things that you need to work on. You will find that it is a start to a new beginning for you to say enough. I don't care what people think anymore. I am doing me right now. I am learning how to be kind to myself. I am learning how to show myself the way without always feeling like I need permission to enhance my own life.

I know that this might sound strange, but it is good to help yourself out of darkness than wait around for someone to rescue you. If someone offers to help you, that ok, but do not set yourself up by waiting around for someone to give you a hand or show you the way. Finding your way through life is never an easy task but it is worth it when you go through the daily challenges and growth on your own terms, you will appreciate your journey much more.

Accepting Yourself Fully

As you get older you should begin to start feeling more comfortable in your skin. Every one of us has imperfections so do not focus on your imperfections. Learn to just simply love you. Accept who you are. Take time out to know yourself, that can sometimes be a challenge if you are not truly into yourself. Sometimes if we are not careful, we will spend more time helping our friends than ourselves… Take on yourself as a project first, and only after you have fixed yourself, then you should allow others in your sacred private space.

Protect your space because it helps to protect you. When you are accepting of yourself, you will begin to feel more powerful to make changes that align with your own vision, goals, and dreams to raise you up for success, and it does not matter where you are from. Practice self-acceptance by learning how to improve, make changes that are necessary for growth and create a safe space to think, assess and clarify your thoughts about yourself. It is okay to ask yourself, what does being great look like for me in the next 5 years. Even though I love myself and accept myself, does this mean I of to settle? No. It is just that you are thinking ahead and feeling your self-confidence growing. Your confidence and self-acceptance have improved so much, that you now start smiling more and putting all your life pieces together, one goal at a time.

Stop Thinking That You Have the World and Start Learning That You Only Have You

Push yourself and stop thinking that everybody is looking out for you. It is the other way around, you are looking out for yourself, while others are providing support when they can. Remember that the people you are depending on, have goals and dreams too, so if you are waiting around for them to help push your career or give you an opportunity, it may never come.

Be conscious of your thinking. When you are conscious of your thinking, you begin to view your purpose in life differently because you start making plans based on who you must depend on, that is yourself. No, I am not saying that family and friends will leave you stranded, I am saying that you need to learn to carry yourself.

When you stop thinking that you have the world and start learning that you only have yourself, planning becomes even better because survival becomes a part of who you are in the long term, so when those who you love disappoint you, even though it will hurt and you will be angry, it will not break you because you never counted them as a part of your process or pathway to success anyway.

Communication

Learn to communicate with others in a pleasant and positive way. There is no perfect way to communicate our feelings because sometimes we speak in anger or just in passing, and we make comments that may not seem genuine. Watch your body language when interacting with others to make certain that you are not putting out the wrong energy.

Communicate to others how you want to be treated, so they do not become comfortable with treating you how they feel is best. You set the foundation for how you want to be treated and this is with anyone. Do not give others a pass to create their own design of how you should be without your permission because sometimes it is not best for you, but easy for them.

Self-love And Inner Peace

Take time to be honest with yourself about your feelings, so that you can see yourself, even when no one else can. Love yourself because you are special. Love yourself because you belong to yourself. Love yourself because self-love generates inner strength and compassion. It is never too late to start over because life is worth living at any age.

Take time to be expressive with the way you present yourself to the world every day. Let no one tell you, how to look or feel. If it feels right for you, then move with it. Think for yourself, so that your choices are yours and not someone else. People are always going to try and change you. Make you into who they want you to be but that is not ok. Be bold in your choices and be brave after you make them. Always think of ways to win, and never focus on losing. Take ownership of yourself, so that the haters can only hate but they cannot hurt you.

When you find that inner peace, you will know. The things that once bothered you or make you feel obligated to please others, will matter no more. You will learn to tune people out when they are been negative and embrace yourself as you have never done before. Even those who once mattered to you will become null and void. Their words will no longer hurt you because you no longer see them as a factor. They become shrapnel and serve no purpose in your life. You become selective, of who you allow in your personal space. Those who once had an influence over you will be removed from your life because you have cut them off. They will try to return to your life, but the removal process is already complete, and you now see them for who they are.

Once you have cleansed your system of negative people and their fake demeanor, they cannot return to your life, because the space they once occupied, is now taken by inner peace and the pure joy that you have now found, through self-actualization. You have finally discovered yourself and all its beauty.

Be a fan of yourself and make conscious decisions to land on your feet. Listen to your own voice and hear it. Be patient with yourself, even if no one around you cares. It is you that matter. It is your voice that will carry you on your personal journey. It's okay to take note of the advice that others give you but do not allow it to control your vision.

Breathe, it's ok. Take a break if you need to but do not stray from the pathway to success. Be clear about what you want when you pray. Do not ask for things that you are not ready to receive. Give yourself credit for being exceptional and fabulous. Stay humble on your journey, even when your wins are more than you have ever imagined. Do not be selfish, share your formula for success with others.

Inner Beauty

My inner beauty and my outer beauty are close friends because one shows off my physical self and the other brings out my inner beauty, so that I can be a ray of light, that brightens up the universe. I spent years wearing make up on my face, which kept breaking me out and causing me to have acne on my face. I thought it make me more beautiful, not realizing at the time, that I am already naturally beautiful. It took my adult life at the age of 30 to stop wearing makeup, because my barber, told me to try and go without make up for a month. I took his advice and stop wearing makeup permanently, after realizing that I was more beautiful without it.

I have taken control of letting my feelings about me, be first by pushing forward, what my version of beauty looks like. I am more confident now, in myself than ever before. I feel stronger, beautiful, confident, focus and powerful in how I present myself and the way that I live. I want to encourage young women all over the world, to focus on self-care and self-love. Do not focus on what others think of you. You matter all the time, not some time.

Everywhere I go, every journey that I travel, I try to teach women and men to trust their inner beauty and allow it to shine through. The inner beauty is more than feelings, it is a sense of belonging and meaning of existence. Knowing who you are from within is very important. You must understand yourself and what your needs are. What makes you special. What lies inside of you, that the world has yet to see. You get to decide what you share with the world and how you show. Let your inner beauty shine because it makes your outer beauty even much more attractive.

Let no one decide what your beauty should look like. Be creative, fearless, confident, and even sometimes mysterious. Face the world with bravery and stand tall in your beauty. Own it. Your personal portrait belongs to you.

Taking Risk

Never allow your inner fear to keep you from reaching for your dreams and building yourself up. Give yourself an opportunity to win. You may not always win but trying is everything because it exposes you to new horizons that can help make a difference in your life. That difference can be your breakthrough into something wonderful. It is ok to set goals for yourself and work on them, one by one. Do not set your lifetime table on the beliefs of others. Look at what your goals mean to you. How will your goals affect your life and what you feel, your purpose is on this earth?

Throughout my life, as I grow from a teenager to a young adult and young adult to the woman that I am today, I have heard more negative opinions of me, than positive from people that I trust. Well, look at me today. I have accomplished more than many hoped for me. I am still reaching for the stars, as I work through life. I never give up and I still set goals for myself, each day. I work on one goal at a time. It could be a personal goal, career goal, financial goal, or spiritual goal. I set those goals based on my standards, not the standards of others.

Please understand, that I do not always reach my goals at the set timetable, but I never give up. I sometimes change the direction of the goal because it no longer seems practical, but I never give up. I restructure my plans and work through them. I have tried a few things in life, that did not go my way immediately, but I never allow that to kill my spirits. Starting over is not a bad thing if you know the pathway that you are trying to follow. One of the things I have always made certain to do is to Lead in my life and not follow. I allow no one, I do not care who it is to dictate how I eat, where I sleep, or how I cook the food that I buy.

When you allow people to take a power of position in your life, they begin to control your every movement and that could ultimately destroy you if you are not careful. Do not allow the insecurities of others to control your way of thinking or how you live. Bullies get their power from praying in the fear of others. Bullies themselves are going through their own insecurities. Take the risk of shutting the bully down, by standing up for yourself.

Bullies are not just in schools, churches, and at work. They are in our own families. They get nasty at family meetings when they do not want to hear the other person speak. They get nasty at family dinners when they have others making them feel that they are powerful. They get nasty and rude if they feel that others will encourage and back their disrespectful behavior towards you or others within the family. Take the risk and remove bullies from your life, regardless of what role they play in your life.

Every story that is worth telling, came with a risk. Every path we take in life is a risk. Do not stand still on your dreams just because it feels uncomfortable to try. Most of the time, those uncomfortable feelings are there because you do not know, what winning feels like and you are afraid of what you might achieve.

Deciding What Works for You

What career is going to make more money but not the career that could make us happy. You get to a place in your life and realize that you are living someone else's dream. You are living someone else's dream because you spent your life worrying about what others wanted for you and not what you wanted for yourself. You start wondering what that person may think of you when they do not matter. You matter. It is your life. The decisions that you make belongs to you. Stop sharing your goals and dreams with people. Keep your goals and dreams to yourself because their thoughts may not be favorable of you. Too often we come across people who are fake and living the life of a pretender.

Do not be fooled by those who seek to destroy your dreams. Decide what you want and work through your process with a clear focus of what it will take, to move you closer to your goals. Every morning that you rise from a sleep, you should be grateful for another day. Take that day and use it to make conscious decisions to land on your feet. Make your positive mark on the world. Do not be a destroyer. Be a builder and an innovator. Even when no one sees your vision, keep looking at it head on, with hope. Your success will come, even if it is at the end of the race. Remember, every race is run differently therefore the ending will not be the same. Even if the same athlete wins the race repeatedly, he or she will not always run the same race. Each match is unique. I never mind being unique growing up. I have my own walk, talk, smile, looks and uniqueness about me. I am special and so are you.

The Big Picture

When we are satisfied with our success, we are supposed to celebrate our hard work and dedication. Sometimes we do not take time to enjoy our success. We make all the conscious decisions, we landed on our feet and then we keep working and working to no end. We become a prisoner of our own success. We are afraid to take a break, in fear that we will become forgotten by those who support us and those who want to see us fail.

We find it hard to say no to the next opportunity in fear that we may not get asked again. We keep a close eye on the competition and allow ourselves to worry over those who do not have the talent to beat us. They are just existing, while we are thriving. They cannot beat you; you have made it. You have arrived. They are standing on the sideline waiting to see your next move. It is your show. It was always your show.

Take time to assess where you are in each chapter of your life. There is nothing wrong with changing careers are feeling like you have done enough of one thing and want to try another. It is all about been bold in your thinking and taking change of your life. A career change can bring you even greater success. Every chapter of your life do not of to be the same. Every chapter of your life has a place, so give it life.

Remember that you are writing your life story so keep it

real with yourself. No one is perfect. Therefore, your story will not be perfect. It will show your ups and downs. Your wins and losses. Your highs and your lows. It will show your character. Make your story mean something by assessing and evaluating the big picture and embracing the wins and the losses. Everything that brought you to this point, have helped to shape you.

Never Giving Up

Sometimes life's challenges take us to places in her minds that we do not want to go. We stop chasing our dreams because we feel defeated. Do not panic. You are not unique. It happens to the best of us.

When you find yourself in those situations, look deep inside and go to that happy place that will help you become calm, cool, and collected. Never allow your current situation, to define what you will become. It is not about what is going on in your life now. It is about your next step and redefining your goals, to get you back on track.

Defeat is never something easy to deal with. It is hurtful, painful and it brings on distress and you begin to question yourself. There are people around, who will also begin to whisper about your lost and disappointment. Pay them no attention, move on your own time. Your destiny belongs to you, not the haters or the nay Sayers. Self-doubt will set in if you let it. Take charge of your own pathway through life, even when it gets difficult.

Sometimes the opportunities that looks like a sure thing can be the worst for you. If you missed it, maybe it was not your time to shine or it would have held you back from greater and better opportunities that God has in store for you. Take the lost and move with faith. Believe that the next opportunity is not only greater and better but will bring you success beyond your wildest imagination. Remember, your friend's dreams are not yours. Your family members cannot determine what works for you. It is your goals, your choice, your movement, your opportunity, your ambition, your purpose, vision, and your destiny. Believe in yourself. You must always be your biggest fan. Always your number one cheerleader.

Stay On Task

We lose focus when too many things and people are added to our process. With success comes more challenges and problems. Success also brings unwanted attention and fake people around you, who are trying to keep you from moving forward by creating distractions for you.

It is important to keep your goals in the forefront of your mind and realize your own dreams and goals. You need to be solid in your convictions. Know yourself and your own possibilities. Do not allow anyone to dictate what your future should look like.

Do not get me wrong, you can take advice from others, however, do not allow them to shape your career path or your vision. If an interest on your list of goals do not pan out or seems challenging now, put it on the bottom of the list and keep it moving. Do not stop because someone tells you to. Stop because that is what you want to do.

Make every year your best, by accomplishing at least one goal on your list. Every conscious decision that you make, is taking you one step closer to accomplishing your dreams and realizing your full potential.

Have Something to Believe In

What do you believe in? What makes you get up in the morning? What do you hope for? It is my believe that when you have a purpose it helps to move your forward in life. Your purpose helps you to define your goals therefore your goals are a result of your purpose. A man or woman with no purpose seek after things that are not good because you become lost looking for things that are not there.

Our beliefs often stem from what we were taught as children and then it spills over into our adult life. The challenge sets in, when we try to break away from what we are taught to create our own ideals of what we see as our truth and we allow the people in our lives such as boyfriends, friends, coworkers, associates, etc., to influence our decision making.

Then comes turmoil. You become conflicted because you are giving your power to others without fulling thinking things through. Know what you believe in and stay true to it. It is ok to turn off the television and read a book to broaden your horizon. It is ok search your soul. Soul searching is good because it also can bring healing and resolution. share your truth.

Learn to Forgive!

Forgiveness is a beautiful thing. Never worry about what the other person or persons think about you. If they bruise you, learn to let them go. Understand even though forgiveness is a good thing, that does not signify that it is easy. Forgiveness is for you, so that you can go on and be at peace. Holding something in your heart, can stifle your growth because that hurt will sit on your and destroy your mind.

Forgiving someone is not an indication of reconnecting. It is simply setting yourself free of the person, hurt, pain, destruction, betrayal and removing clutter from your life. Take back your power by letting the enemy go.

Forgiveness does not signify that the door is open for those who hurt you to come back into your life. It is an opening for you to become stronger and to add more meaning to your life by allowing yourself to look towards making new connections and moving forward to new possibilities and exciting opportunities just waiting around the corner for you.

Keep in mind, that forgiveness is voluntary therefore you are choosing to let go of bitterness and negativity that may have kept you from realizing your true full potential. Never let anyone steal your joy. Take back your power by making conscious decisions to land on your feet.

Taking Advantage of Opportunities Even When They Seemed Small

Do not reject opportunities just because they seem lower than what you expected. If it falls in line with what you want to do with your life, make it work for you. Take small opportunities and expand on them by getting creative and innovative. Every opportunity brings something new to your life. The outcome is up to you. Ask yourself, what can I do to make this work for me?

Every opportunity should be used to elevate you to the next phase of your life. It does not always need to be about money. It can be about setting the stage for your next big golden opportunity. It could be setting up your next situation that will turn into the perfect avenue for great favors to come upon your life.

Sometimes we look too deep into the opportunity and we miss the main reason why it was placed before us. We want perfection but sometimes our opportunities come to us in a rush and we of to grab a hold it quickly. Have you ever heard someone say, I have accomplished allot but I have not taken time out to enjoy it? It is not because they do not want to enjoy their success, it is because it all happened so fast, that they are still in process mode.

When you invest in yourself, and have laid the groundwork for success, there is no perfect timing for your labor to come in. It happens when you least expect it. Here is my advice to you, while you labor and invest in yourself, trust yourself and begin to think ahead about how you will enjoy your success, when it comes.

What Does Success Look Like for You

Are you satisfied with where you are in life? If not, why not? Do you have control over your own life? Who is in control of your life? If you are not? Then who?

For you to know what success feels like, you need to have a sense of what happiness looks like for you. Sometimes we tend to view the happiness of others as what our happiness should look like.

Your list of goals should reflect what you hope for. Do not be concerned about those who are doing better than you. Focus on the progress that you have made and how it makes you feel. Measure your success based on where you are coming from and how much more you would like to achieve. Your success is about you. Give yourself credit for trying. It is ok to critique yourself but do not be hard on yourself.

Do not be concerned about who got to the finish line first. Run your own race. You will get there and when you are satisfied you will know, what success look like for you. Do not allow your past failures to affect how you see yourself.

Changing Direction and Moving Forward

It is never the end just because you have made the conscious decision to make a career change or reorganize your plans to shift your life focus onto something else that interest you. You have the right to make decisions that enhance your life and career growth. You are going to have those who question your choices but do not allow their doubts are questions to stop you. Use doubts to strengthen your pathway to success. Even those who you work with, live with, sit and conversate with, will try to stop your growth and question your choices. They do not matter. You matter because you should be your first motivation.

How often do you sit and review your plans that you made 2 years or 5 years ago? Always review and adjust as needed because with growth comes changes and improvements. Those who pretend to be perfect and have plans that do not need adjustments, are often times not keeping it real with you. Learn to build on your own strength that God gave you. Never stop planning, never stop creating. Always consider yourself a student so that you can continue to grow and elevate to the next level of your life.

When You Are Not Chosen

Sometimes you have it all planned out and then life happens. Its ok. As long as you are breathing, you can try again and again. Never give up. Think of all the people before you, who have paved the way for you to have an opportunity, to be exposed to all the wonderful career pathways that we now have to consider. Ask yourself, can I waste any opportunity? The answer should be no. All opportunities are important. Opportunities are given to you, so that you can prove to yourself that you are just as capable as those before you and those who will come after you to be great. Do not give up on yourself. Take control of your own possibilities. Look at what you have accomplished, large or small and build from there.

You are not always going to be chosen. That is ok. Be happy for the person that won and use their win as an inspiration to continue working at your own goals. Maybe that opportunity was not for you. Focus on your wins and your movement to be great. Do not be derailed by what others have accomplished. Remember, if it were to be yours, it would have been given to you. Choose yourself. Your empowerment will come based on how you feel about you. Love yourself enough and be your own fan. When you love yourself, it will show in all your doings. Even how you interact with the enemy.

Leaving People Behind

Never feel bad because you leave an old friend behind. There is nothing wrong with that. Sometimes the company you keep, can hold you back and keep you from your destiny. They do not share your joy and hungry for success. They do not see the possibilities in life that can change you or your community. They want to focus on remaining stagnant and keep focusing on the past, never looking towards the future. Often times the friends you leave behind, need to stay there, and do not move forward with you. You value their existence, but you do not value their offerings. For example, your views are different. Their focus is negative. Their upward movement is stagnant because they do not see their purpose and if they see it, they do not value it.

The people you left behind; will always have something to say about your growth with a negative undertone because they are bitter. Leave them in their bitterness and keep walking forward. Never let them steal the joy that you have acquired through hard work and perseverance.

Give yourself a break.

34

The End.

Made in the USA
Monee, IL
07 July 2026

56549805R00021